AF372553

Career Biography is for Senior High School Students only because you are at your decision point, "What do I do when I leave High School." You are going to have to either start earning money or attend college, which costs money. As you will see, I got a job right away, took care of my Military obligation, went back to work, and then took some college courses in line with my career choice.

Work is a four-letter word, but **work is fun!** (did I lose you already?) Okay, **work** you like to do is fun! (got you back?) **Work** in your chosen career field is fun. Lots of fun. Let me tell you about how I found a career field I liked to **work** in.

I lived in Shorewood, Wisconsin in the home on the right until I was 12-years old. During that time I saw the movie, The Young Thomas Edison. I was fascinated by

what he could do with simple things like pulleys.

My brother and I had a bedroom, which my dad built upstairs, behind those two top windows. I was 10 when I ran wires from our bedroom to the dining room buffet downstairs. I connected the wires in our bedroom to a 6-volt battery and to a doorbell, and downstairs to a pushbutton. My mother would push the button in the dining room downstairs causing the

bell to ring in our bedroom when it was time for us to get up for school. She could also talk to us through the family's intercom I wired between the floors.

A metal wagon we had, just like the one shown on the next page, rusted through and lost its wheels in the back.   I found some 2x4s behind the garage and built a wagon frame 7 feet long with "spikes" (I called them, nails I bought from the hardware store with my allowance money). Then I added the wheels from the old wagon to the frame.

Since the new wagon was so long, I added levers on each side with ropes connected to the steering

wheels up front. You
had to steer with the
levers, which took some
time to get used to.

When Fall came and the
street gutters were filled
with leaves, I added a
plywood plow to the
front, again controlled
with a lever. We
plowed the leaves into
nice piles for the neighbors.

At Halloween time, I added a small house and a hay
stack, dressed my friends in white sheets and we
pushed the affair almost a mile to Shorewood High
School to enter a Halloween parade costume contest.
We won first prize.

My dad took me to the largest
hotel in Milwaukee where he
worked as Chief Electrician.
There I saw the elevator room
with its bank of relays,
clicking away. I begged my
dad to get me a relay. After 3
months he brought one home
for me and handed it to me
with no explanation. I blew a
few fuses until I understood

how it worked. Then I discovered how one could cause a relay to latch – stay on – with the push of a (momentary-switch) button. It "remembered" that I had pushed the button, and that simple discovery started me in the direction of my career.

We moved when I was 12 to what was then the country. From our second floor bedroom (again which my Dad built) I ran 1,000 feet of wire, which I had acquired, from our house to a friend's house. Using the same intercom mentioned earlier, we could talk even when the weather was bad.

At 15 I left home to attend St. Lawrence College in Mt. Calvary, Wisconsin (now called St. Lawrence Seminary High School) where I studied physics and wrote short stories for the school's publication.

In the 4th floor Physics Department I constructed a phono oscillator, connected a long antenna to it, which I tossed out of the window. I connected a microphone and phonograph player to the circuit and broadcast like a disk jockey throughout the building.

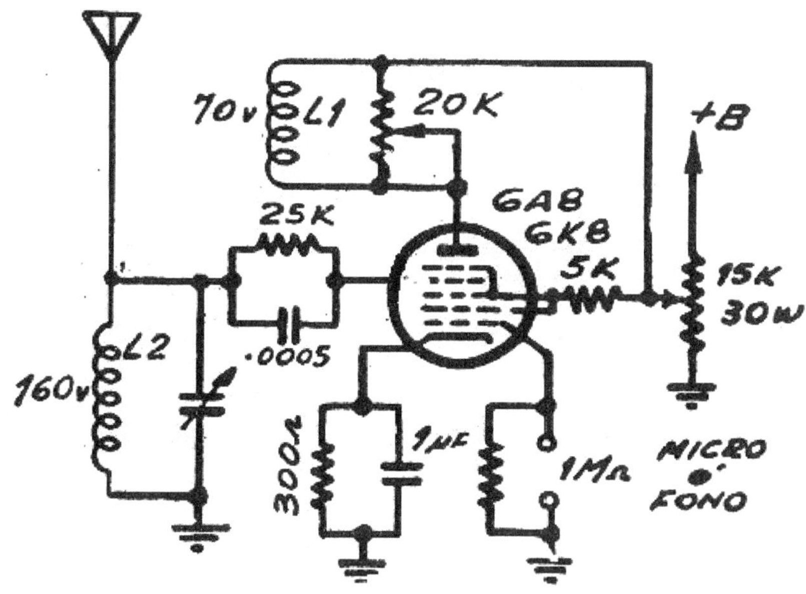

In Home Room, instead of studying, I constructed a telescope at my desk, while hiding behind my books, to look out over the land that called to me.

After three years I left to continue schooling at Don Bosco Technical High School in Paterson, New Jersey. While attending the electronics class, I worked with a French student teacher to install a 30 foot tower on top of the 3-story building, adding an amateur radio antenna to the top. A dangerous venture (no safety equipment), but fun.

I graduated from High School and the school's electronics course. I left the school, taking a bus back to Milwaukee, and **I remember having a strong intention to develop electrical or electronic products for the average consumer as a career choice**.

I came home and immediately was hired by a television repair store. I learned to service electronic organs and focused on that for two years. At that time I joined the Airforce Reserve and spent the next 6 months at Texas and Colorado airbases.

When I returned from Air Force training, I serviced electronic organs another year for Larry's TV. I enjoyed going from home to home, meeting people and getting their electronic organs working again. One time it was the home of a surgeon. He decided to watch me. I opened the back of his very expensive electronic organ like the one in the photo. To find the problem, I had to cut some of the wires and solder in new parts. This guy, used to cutting open humans, said, "I can't watch anymore, it's making me too nervous," and he left the room.

I took some courses at Marquette School of Engineering. **I encourage you to enroll in a college and take courses that will help you with your chosen career.**

At 23, I started the Electromatic Corporation with two electrical engineers. We acquired the organ service and also began to develop electronic products such as the keyless electronic combination ignition switch and keyless home lock shown below.

I also designed and built a trailer taillight system which allowed you to hookup the taillights of a trailer by just taping photocells to the taillights of the pulling vehicle. If brake lights appeared on the taillight of the pulling vehicle, brake lights appeared on the trailer taillights. If it was a blinking light for a turn signal, the same appeared on the trailer. I got my first patent.

A year later, I sold the company to an automotive accessory manufacturer in West Allis, Wisconsin, and went to work for them as an electronics design engineer (remember, I had no Degree). The new company lacked a viable marketing plan for electronic automotive accessories, and I left to join Norland Associates, a professional engineering, product development consulting firm in Fort

Atkinson, Wisconsin where I worked as an Account Manager for two years.

My principal client at Norland Associates was Burgess, a paint sprayer, battery charger and lawn and garden manufacturer. The first project I did for Burgess was a lather dispenser for washing your hands or even shaving. It used an ordinary bar of soap, and by turning the crank, it produced a rich lather. While working for Norland I took a course in

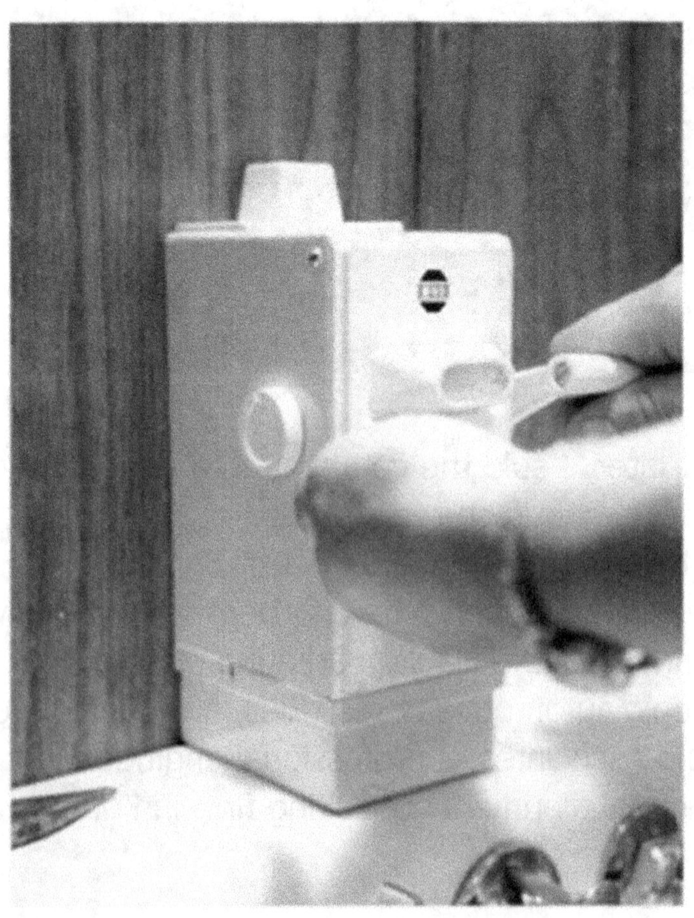

Physics at the University of Wisconsin, Whitewater. I needed to know physics in my chosen career.

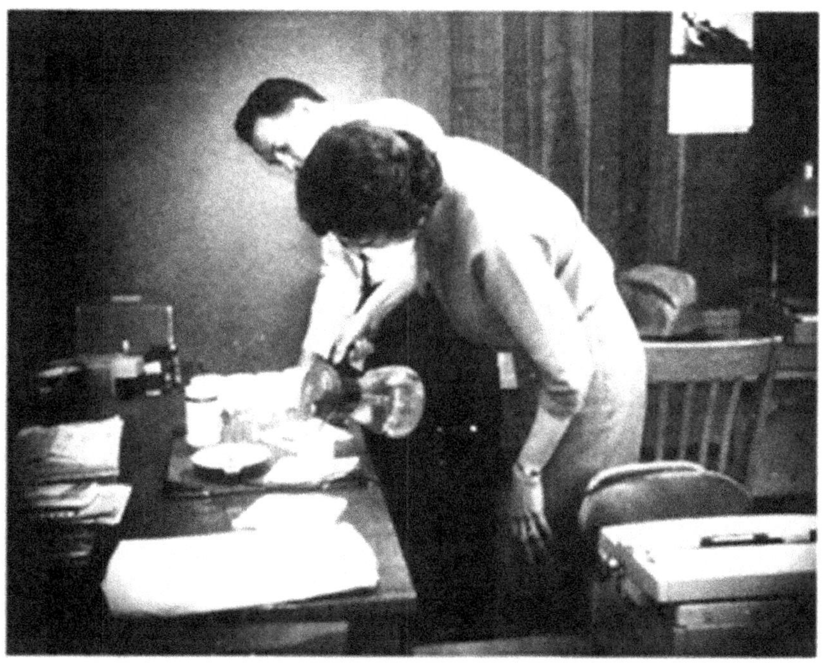

That's the engineering company's secretary pouring an instant cup of coffee from a product I designed. The liquified instant coffee was in the cover of the carafe. You heat the water, then touch a button and you can pour out a cup of coffee like magic. The President of the company also designed one. Mine worked, his didn't.

Burgess was considering entering the electric housewares market which interested me (fit my career choice). When their Board of Directors voted against the move, I joined National Presto Industries, in Eau Claire Wisconsin, as a Project Engineer where I worked for three years developing product after product, a corn popper, a fondue, a shoe polisher, a vibrating hairbrush. While I was there, I wrote articles for Popular Electronics and Design News. I have every one of those products below in my "museum."

I was offered an opportunity to acquire an electronics distributor/dealer franchise, so I moved my family to Rochester, Minnesota and opened the first Team Electronics store.

That's one of my salesmen with two cheerleaders. Since the electronics store chain was called "Team," I thought cheerleaders should be part of the team. I paid them to work in the store once in a while. They both were in High School.

In a year and a half, the store was running and quite profitable, but I wanted to get back into product research and development, back to the career of my choice.

I talked again with National Presto and was immediately rehired this time as a Senior Project Engineer. I received numerous assignments.

National Presto's Guardian Service division in Los Angeles, California was looking for a new product line to sell through their direct sales organization. I received the assignment to develop an entire line of home security devices for the division.

Some of the products were to be manufactured in Hong Kong and I monitored the pilot production there. When the product line was in production, Guardian Service asked me to join them as a Product Manager in Los Angeles, California.

After three years I was appointed General Manager of the division. But I missed product research and design.

By chance, Norland Associates contacted me and asked me to return to the consulting firm as Account Manager and Director of Marketing. I accepted and developed a variety of new products for clients.

One of the products was probably the first robotic vacuum cleaner. There were no small, powerful batteries back then, so we found a way to keep it plugged in.

Another client asked us to develop a remote control for outboard motors. We asked some teenagers to test it, and they stood on the seat and flew around the lake using it like a powered surfboard.

For Burgess, again my client, I designed a keyless door lock, and for the Caterpillar company, I designed an in-the-cab alarm, volume adjustable.

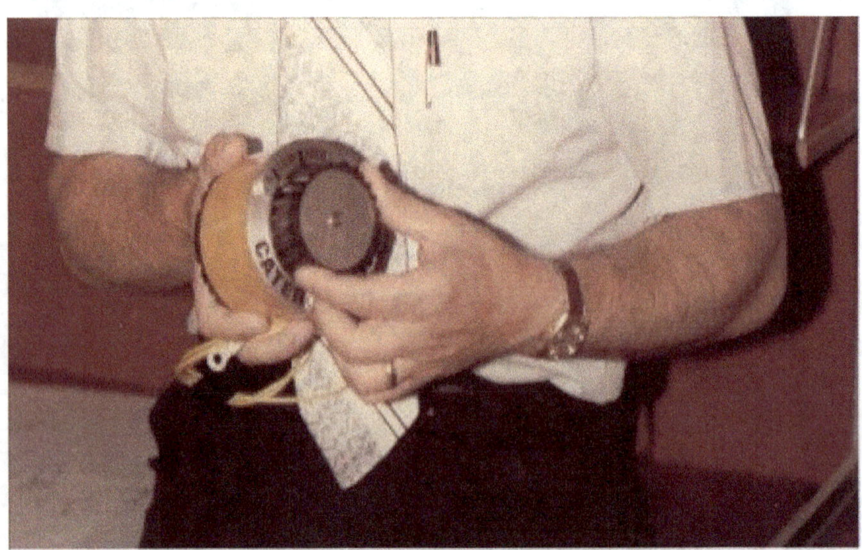

Norland's parent company, Norland Instruments, was sold to the Cordis Corporation and Norland Associates moved to Janesville, Wisconsin. Burgess was again my client and they asked me to join their company as Director of Engineering. I worked for Burgess for six years and was promoted over that time to Vice President of Engineering, Vice President of Operations and finally as Executive Vice President. I met Kim there.

Again, I was responsible for many new products being placed into production. I received a patent on every one of those lawn and garden products on the right.

Did I thus far enjoy the career I chose, and did I enjoy the work? Absolutely. The work was fun, every minute of it.

Then the real fun began. Product research engineering **consulting**. Kim and I started **Intresearch** (International Research).

Variety! You don't know what a new client will ask you to create and develop next.

That's an ultrasonic fault detector. If it is steel (I beams, girders etc.) and it has a crack in it which may cause a catastrophic failure, this fault detector will find it. I designed

everything you can see. The electronics team did the insides.

On the right is a special purpose, **self-maintaining**, fax machine. The product was originally used to take orders from salesmen in the field and transfer them directly to a company's computer system.

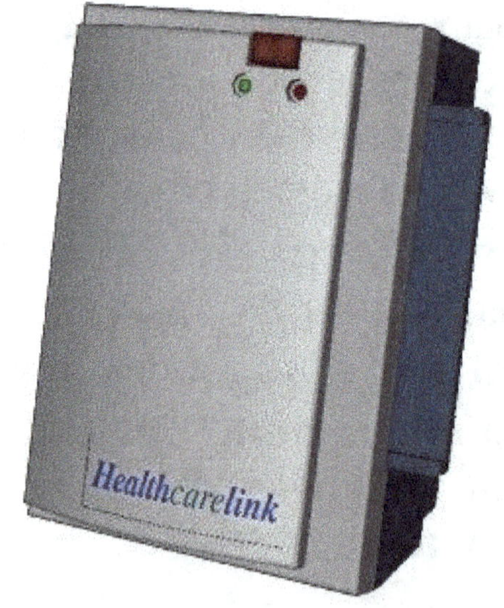

To maintain itself, every time you touched the red button to send in an order, the device would, 1. instantly look itself over, and if it found a problem, it would literally change the software to override it, 2. if it could not fix the problem, it would automatically call a remote computer which had more capabilities to fix problems, and 3. if the remote computer could not fix the problem; it would automatically print out a Fed Ex label to have a replacement shipped to wherever the faulty device was located.

Later, Healthcarelink used the machine as a **telemedicine** device to send patient health data to a remote computer for graphing and forwarding to healthcare providers.

For Rayovac, my team and I designed two dramatic flashlights.

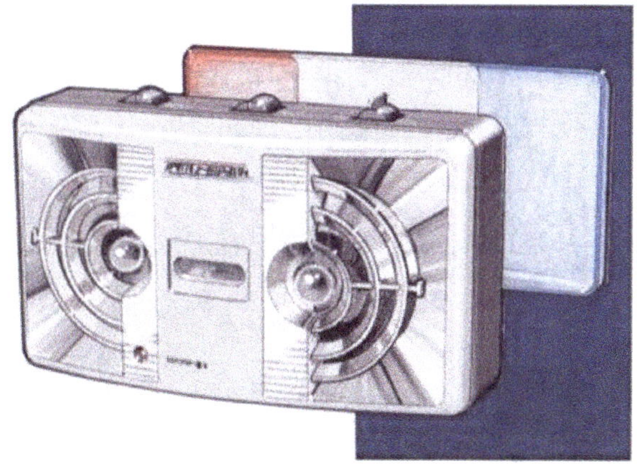

The one on the right threw two beams. With the controls on the top, you can get both beams to hit the object you want to look at for double the brightness. And when you do that, the flashlight will tell you exactly how far away the object is from you.

You have never seen them on the market, because they outperformed the big clunky lantern flashlight on the left, which they had just tooled.

I believe the phone below may have been the first touch-screen telephone. We built three models for Mytel, a Canadian telephone company, and yes, you could make selections by touching the screen.

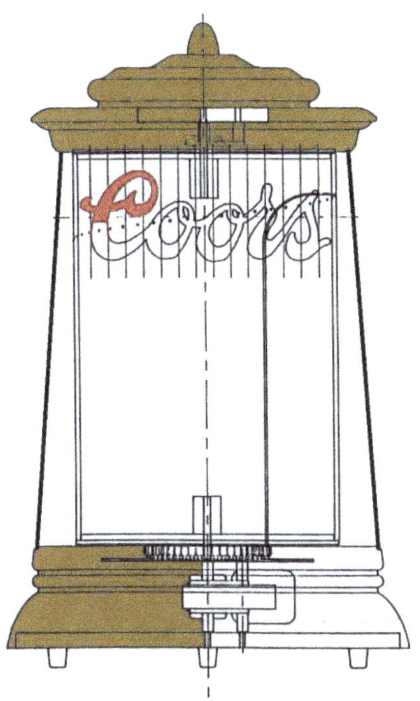

For a Coors consultant we designed this spinning display to sit on tavern bars . It would gradually write out the word Coors. **Spooky**.

And for a company that made these popular phone booths, we designed a three-station phone booth with a spinning advertisement on top and advertising above the phone on an LCD display. I have the display in my museum.

I designed this half of a wagering terminal; still in use I am told. The teller could sell tickets from this side, and if the screen was flipped up, the buyer could do it themselves on the touchscreen display.

Next was a really neat project. Lots of fun. It was the equivalent of designing a complete dishwasher, except this machine sterilized surgical instruments. I designed and constructed an operating model in the basement of my home.

The sterilizer used a very toxic chemical contained in a cartridge. On the label it said, something like, "If you open this cartridge, you will likely die."

To avoid that, you would insert the cartridge in the machine and close that front cover. To be sure you wouldn't open it during the cleaning process, the cover was kept closed with atmospheric pressure, 15 pounds per square inch. The cover was 24 x 24 inches. Go ahead, calculate the total pressure.

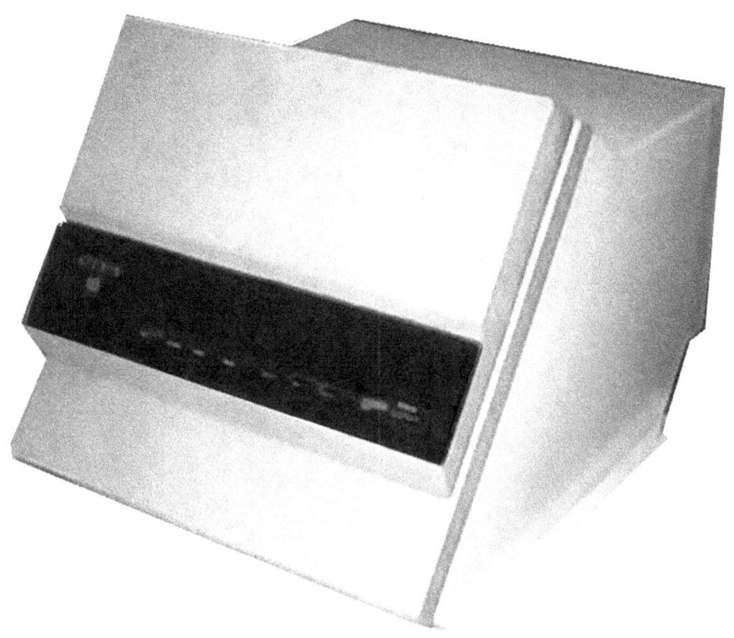

A GE engineer came to me and said, "I'm in trouble. I am designing this Police Radio and I have too many parts going into too little space." I said, "Why don't we put the connecting printed circuit right on the supporting plastic part." "Can we do that?" he asked. "I don't know. Let's try it." You can see the plastic/printed circuit that resulted. GE made 50,000 of those police radios.

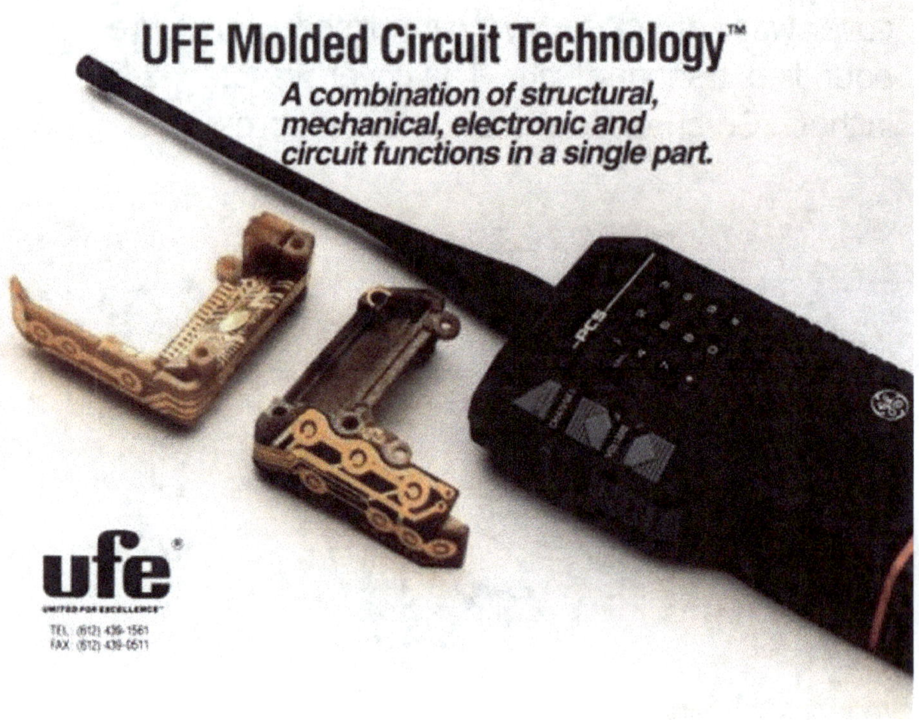

Everyone was selling a lighted mirror. There was nothing new out there. We rendered the lighted mirror on the top of the next page to do more than other lighted mirrors. The women could select colors on a side panel to see if clothing of that color would go with their makeup.

Kim modeled for the rendering, but that does not look like her.

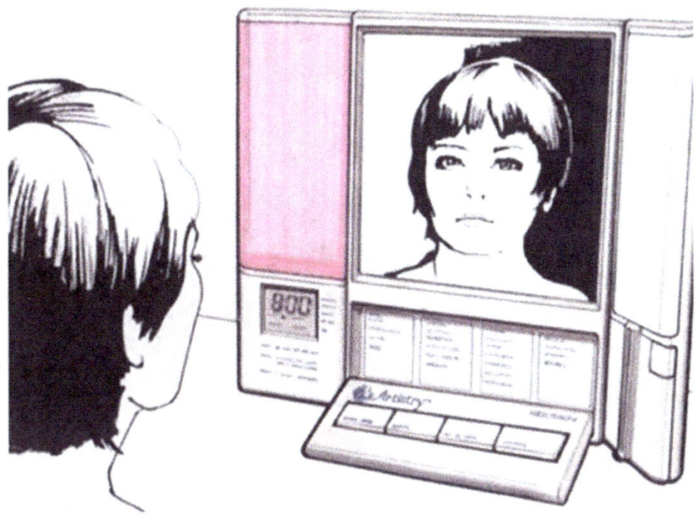

The lighted mirror we finally designed below did even more. It was to be connected to the Internet. Have you heard of the "Internet of Things (IoT)"? Someone halfway around the world was helping this lady put on eye makeup. I don't know who she is.

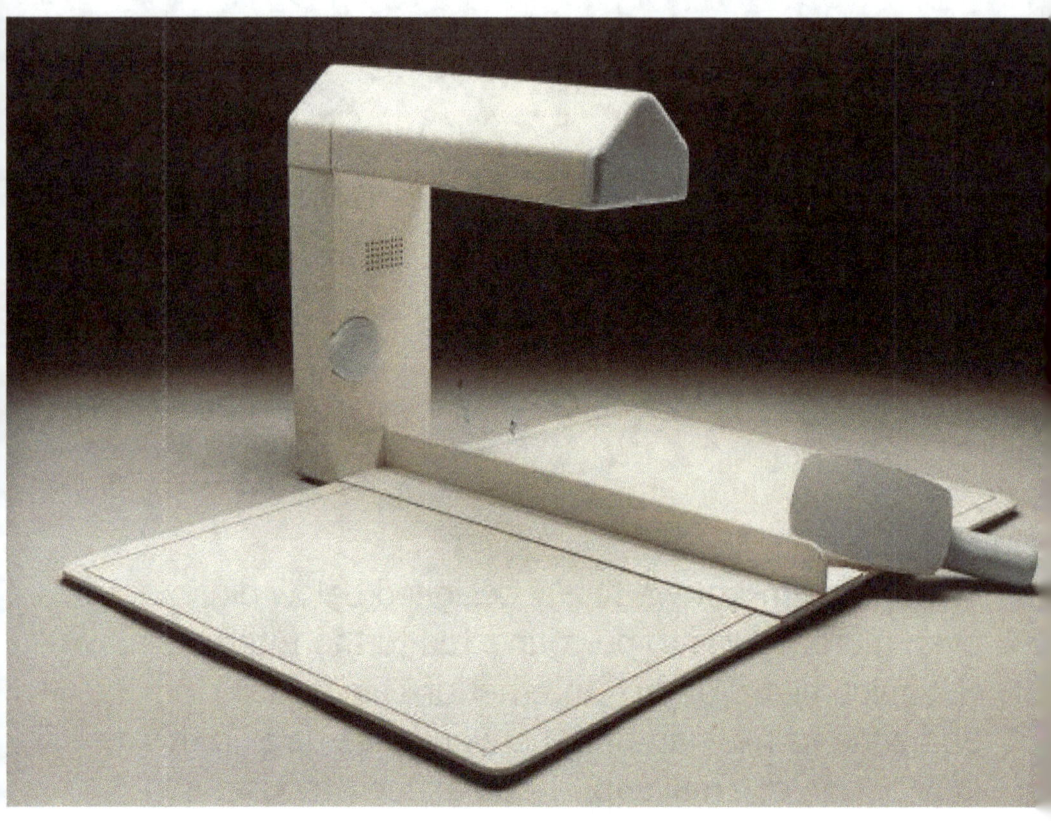

Talking about IoT, you can play this paddle game with the built-in computer, with someone in the room (comes with two paddles) or with someone anywhere in the world. You don't see a ball, do you? The ball was projected optically onto the play table, yet you feel the ball hit the paddle! We made one and as you play it you become convinced there really is a ball going back and forth. Great fun and they paid me to design it.

For GE Communications we designed a police car radio and siren control panel. It was also used by CHiPs, California Highway Patrol, on their motorcycles, so it had to be largely waterproof. Sometimes on the news we would see it on a policeman's motorcycle.

If you want a great knife sharpener, get this one. It was invented by a scientist. I designed it. A doctor friend of mine bought one recently.

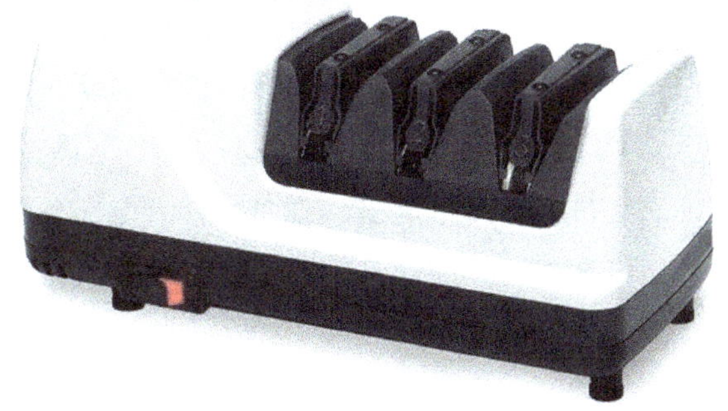

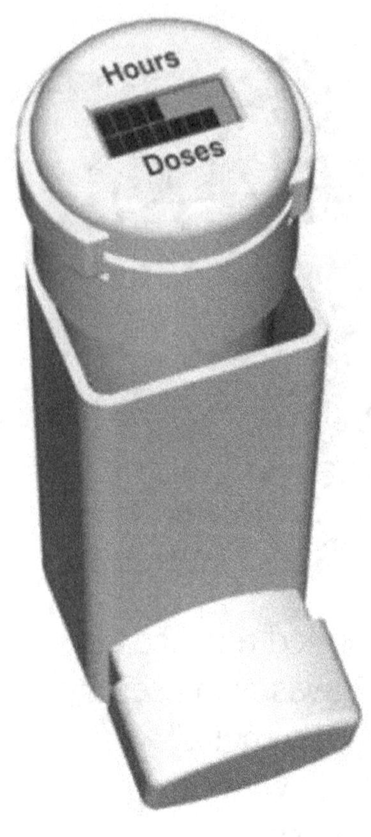

I can't forget this project because I use one every day. I have asthma and I use an inhaler. You are not supposed to use it more often than every 4 hours, and it's quite impossible to know how much is left (now they have a tiny little counter at the bottom of the inhaler – difficult to read).

A marketing firm asked me to design the dose monitor shown on the top of the medication canister. Every time you use it, the "Hours" resets, and the amount, "Doses," is recorded. I wouldn't be without it.

Talking about a fun project, my team and I designed this electric, convection, broiling barbeque grill for Weber. I gained 20 pounds testing it. It cooked a whole chicken in 38 minutes and left it so juicy, they had to warn customers not to spill it when taking it off the grill.

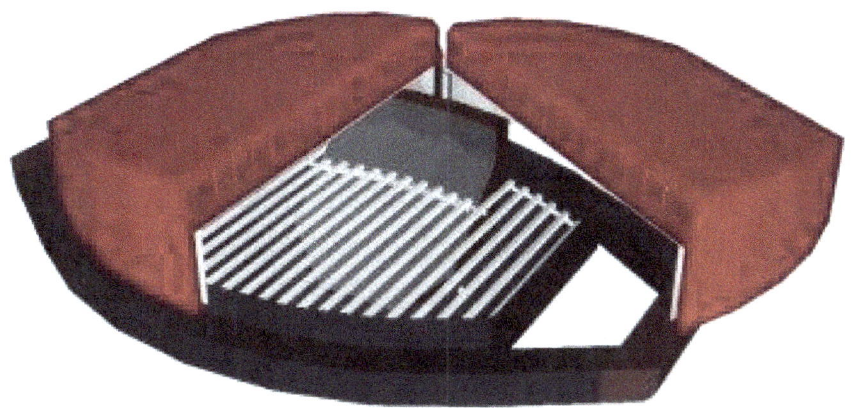

How about an alarm clock, you just have to touch the numbers to set. No going around 59 numbers to get where you want to go, just touch the number you want to change. It operated in three colors, red, green, and white. There's one on my desk and my name is on the patent

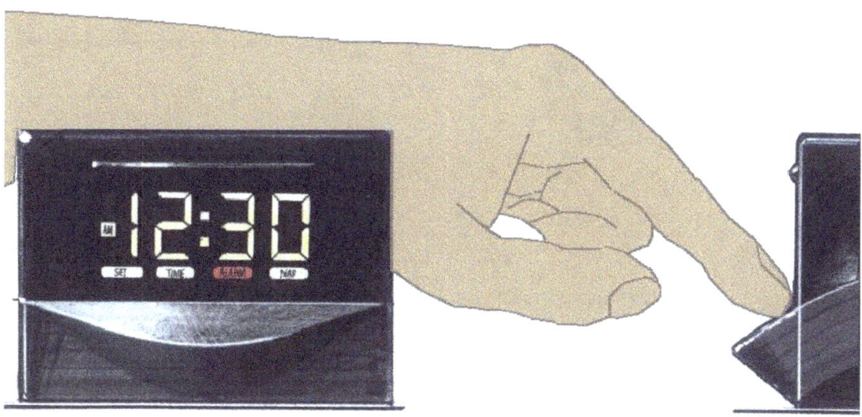

I designed a complete line of boat navigation lights and horn, working with an engineering physicist. The lights were the "best ever tested" by the Coast Guard. The two-mile lights were visible at four miles. Lens segments were ultrasonically welded together. The aluminum disk on top served as a heat sink which dissipated the heat from the high-performance lamp.

We even designed an emergency exit light. During an emergency, the exit sign and the red strip was illuminated all the way down to the floor.

And also, I designed this gas grill control for Weber. On one of my websites you can operate it virtually.

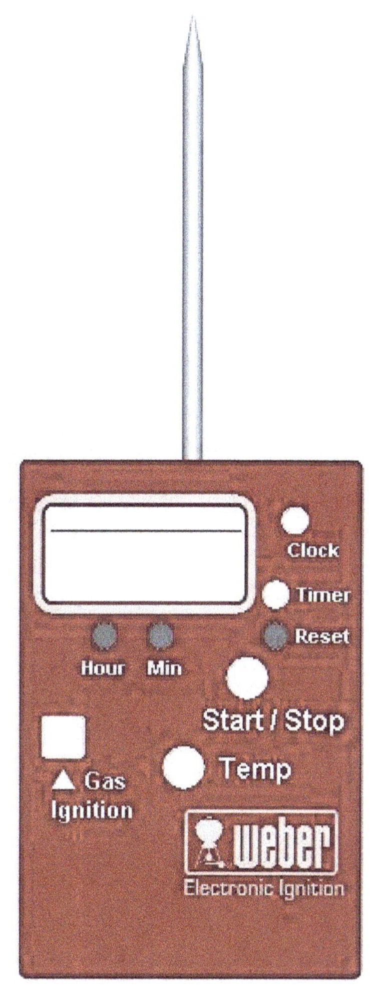

Below is a rough sketch of a potato chip maker/fryer. Shove a potato down the tube, rotate the cover and thin slices of potatoes drop into the hot oil below, held at a precise temperature. After just the right amount of cooking time, the heat shuts off and a basket of potato chips rises above the oil automatically.

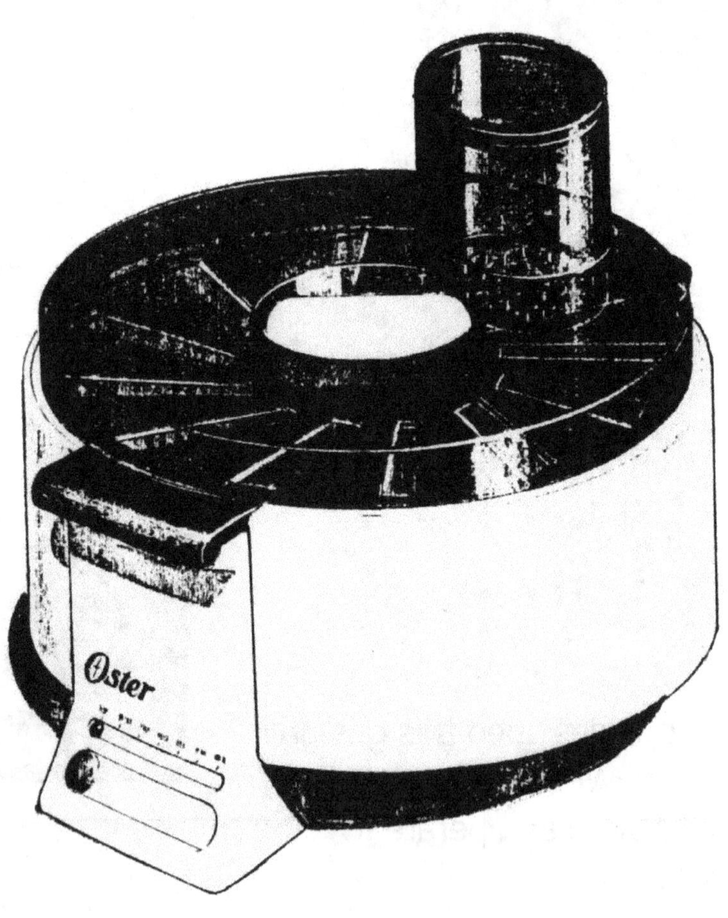

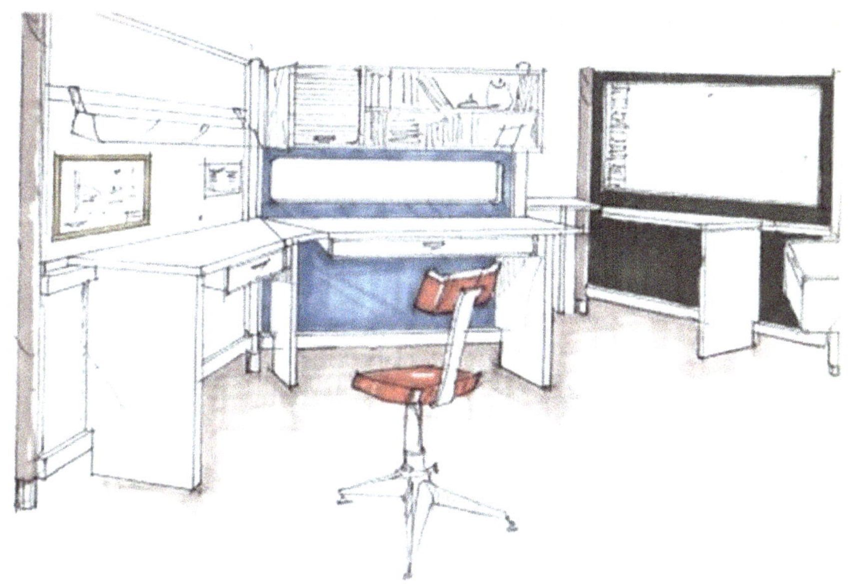

For a Minnesota office station furniture
manufacturer, we designed this office for design
engineers. The computer equipment is not shown,
nor can you see the special bracket we designed to
mount the work surfaces. My Industrial Design
friend and I designed these wall hanging stereo
speakers. They sounded great.

And what am I doing now? Well, I'm working in the medical field, developing electronic products for the average consumer just as I set out to do when I graduated from High School.

Take a look at my favorite and the most important project of my entire career.

The Biosymtec Telemedicine System

The heart of the Biosymtec Telemedicine System is  the **TeleKit™** shown on the left. Its primary purpose is for use in telemedicine visits with healthcare providers.

The **TeleKit** is comprised of three housings all hinged appropriately at the back of the housing.

A U.S. Patent has been applied for covering the TeleKit and the Biosymtec Monitor. A PTC filing will soon follow.

The **Biosymtec TeleKit**
includes:

A multi-function, wireless,
portable camera
(**Camometer™**)

A color LCD touchscreen
display

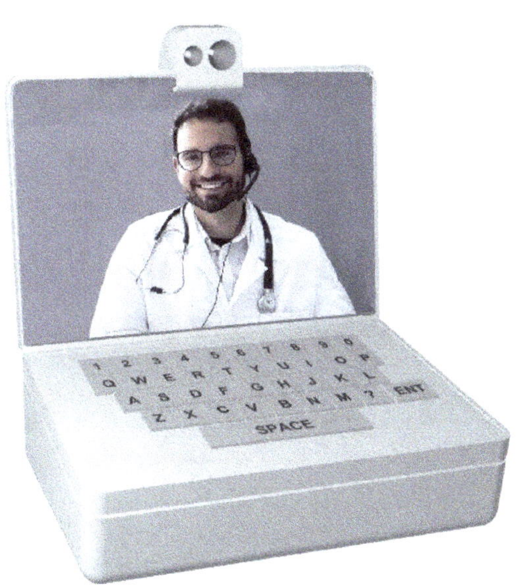

An integrated QWERTY
keyboard

Onboard health data
graphing and display

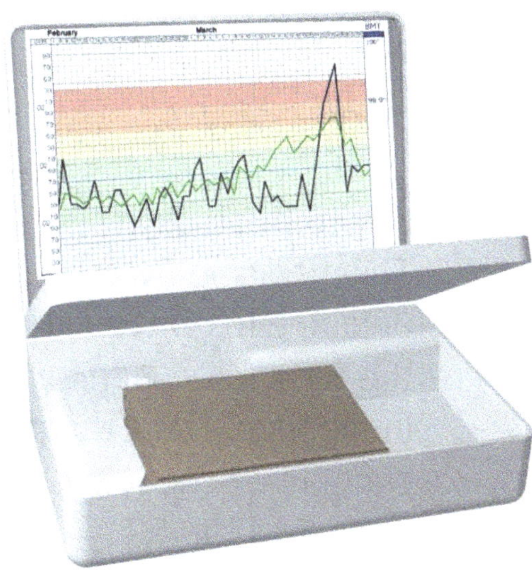

Storage room for the
Camometer and other
telemedicine devices.

An integrated blood
pressure monitor with
upper arm cuff.

The **Camometer** is wireless and rechargeable. It includes an HD video camera, a light source, a microphone and an IR thermometer.

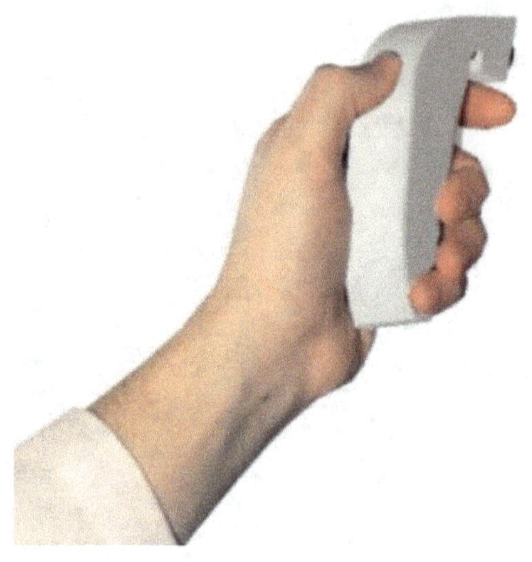

The **Camometer** also recharges wirelessly when mounted on the back of the display where it is secured magnetically.

Key to the Biosymtec Telemedicine System is the unique **Biosymtec Monitor**. Used upon waking, the Biosymtec Monitor's AI algorithm (**Aila™**) immediately tells the patient whether a televist should be scheduled, well before symptoms send the patient to the ER

.

The **TeleKit** can also receive alerts from compatible home security systems, allowing the resident to observe would-be intruders and contact security personnel.

The **Telekit** can be used to Zoom with relatives, especially those concerned with the patient's health and security.

Let me tell you more about the Biosymtec Monitor. This product, when finally in production and on the market, could save the lives of hundreds of thousands of people with asthma, COPD (chronic obstructive pulmonary disease), heart failure and children with cystic fibrosis (CF).

The **Biosymtec Monitor** is kept by the bedside so that it can be used upon waking, before getting out of bed.

The dual probes are placed under the tongue, straddling the frenulum. A special core temperature is taken.

Upon rising the patient blows hard and long through the monitor. An AI algorithm **(Aila™)** delivers immediate results which are shown on the Biosymtec Monitor display. Yes, an AI algorithm I wrote tells the patient whether it is important to schedule a televisit with their doctor.

This patient had better schedule a televisit right away. She may feel perfectly well, but **Aila** knows better.

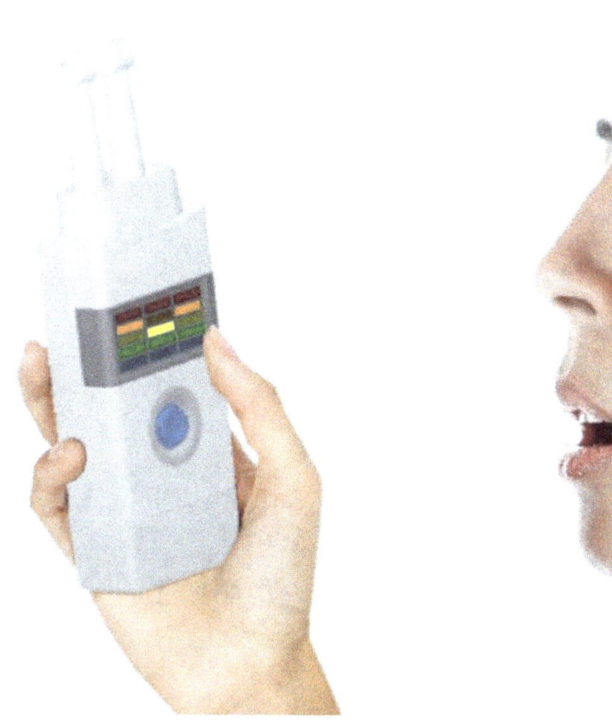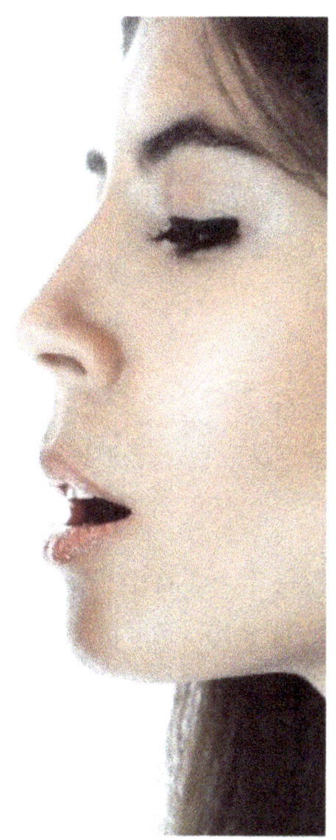

Aila also talks to the TeleKit, and the TeleKit graphs the information **Aila** provides. Here is the graph of a patient that may have been the first in the U.S. to be infected with COVID-19. You can operate it virtually on one of my websites.

The woman on the following page pointing to the graphic is my wife, Kim.

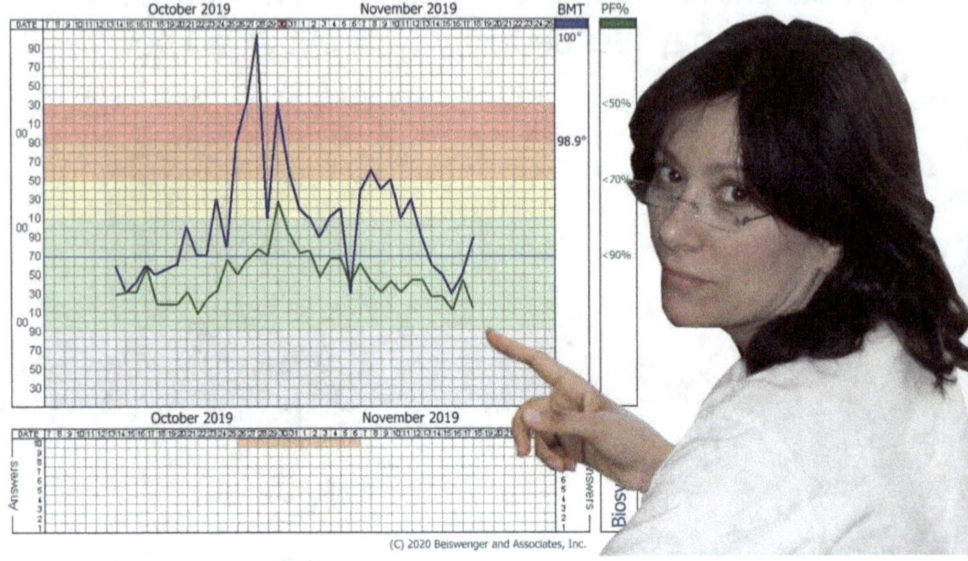

Have I had fun working in my chosen career? Absolutely. **What's yours going to be?** This career list is grossly incomplete, but it may be helpful as a start.

Account executive
Accountant
Agricultural worker
Airline Pilot
Anesthesiologist
Animal breeder
Animator/video game designer
Archeologist
Architect
Auto mechanic
Biomedical engineer
Brand manager

Business development manager
Cafeteria worker
Child welfare social worker
Civil engineer
College professor
Communications manager
Congressional staff
Copywriter
Dental assistant
Design Engineer
Doctor
Entrepreneur/business owner
Fashion designer
Filmmaker
Firefighter
Fisher
Forest and conservation worker
Graphic designer
Human resources manager
Industrial Designer
Industrial Engineer
Journalist
Labor relations specialist
Laboratory technician
Landscape architect
Landscaper and groundskeeper
Lawyer
Licensed clinical social worker
Licensed Nurse Practitioner
Licensed Practical Nurse

Lobbyist
Mail carrier
Marketing assistant
Marketing VP
Microbiologist
Music producer
National park ranger
Nurse
Nursery worker
Palliative and hospice care worker
Paralegal
Photographer
Physical therapist
Physicist
Plumber
Public administrator
Public relations specialist
Real estate agent
Regional sales manager
Rehabilitation counselor
Sales associate
Sales development rep
School counselor
School librarian
School principal
Scientist
Secretary
Singer/songwriter
Social media manager
Software engineer

Special education teacher
Speech pathologist
Substitute teacher
Superintendent
Teacher
Veterinarian
VP of sales
Wind turbine technician
Xray Technician

If a listed career picks your interest, look into it further. More than one may be of interest to you. Now, this is your last year in High School. You should, by the end of this year, be seriously considering a career field before you leave the school and before you sign up for any college courses.

Some careers require a college degree, many don't, especially when you can show job interviewers what you can already do and have already learned. But some college courses, directly related to your chosen career field, will be extremely helpful. They were for me.

I wish you the very best success in your chosen career, and **I hope you have a lot of fun doing the work.**

You can contact me through most of my websites on johnbeiswenger.com.

John Beiswenger
Christian, Author, Engineer